SIMPLE SCIENCE SAYS:
Take One Balloon

Melvin Berger

Illustrated by
G. Brian Karas

SCHOLASTIC INC.

New York   Toronto   London   Auckland   Sydney

To Ellie and Tom

ISBN 0-590-41612-X

Copyright © 1988 by Melvin Berger.
Illustrations copyright © 1988 by Scholastic Books, Inc.
All rights reserved. Published by Scholastic Inc.

12 11 10 9 8 7 6 5 4 3 2 1   8 9/8 0 1 2 3/9

Printed in the U.S.A.   11

First Scholastic printing, October 1988

Contents

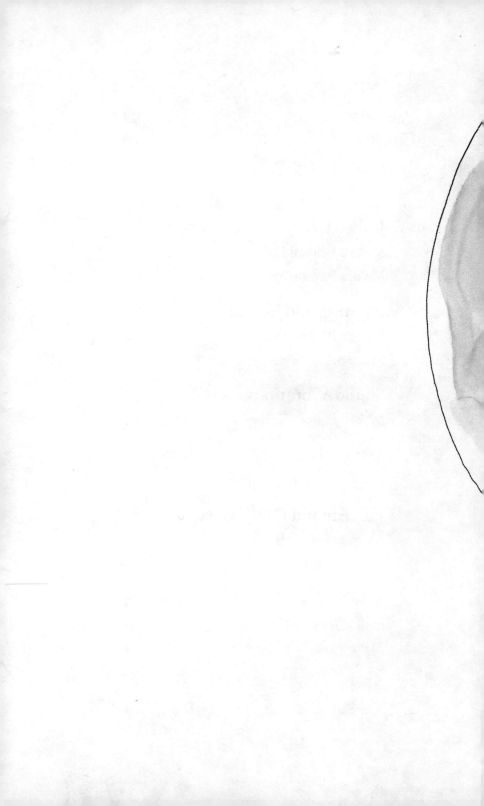

Balloons are great for having fun.
You can punch them…
squeeze them…
throw or twirl them…
string them up…
dribble them.
You can even tuck messages in them
and watch them sail away.

But balloons are also amazing tools of science.
You can make lots of wonderful discoveries
with just one balloon.

So — what are we waiting for?

**SIMPLE SCIENCE SAYS: Take
the balloon from the back of
this book — and let's get started!**

Jet Action

SIMPLE SCIENCE SAYS:
Make a Balloon Rocket

Blow up the balloon.
Pinch the neck tightly
as you take it out of your mouth.
Don't let any of the air escape.
Now, toss the balloon up into the air.
Watch how it darts across the room.

Do you know what makes your balloon fly?
Jet action!
Jet action also sends up rockets into space.
And it sends jet planes around the world.
Let's see how jet action works.

When you blow up a balloon you fill
it with air. The air presses against the balloon
in all directions — forward and backward,
up and down, and against the sides.

When you open the neck, some air escapes.
There is less pressure in that direction.
But the rest of the air keeps
pressing against the balloon.
The inside pressure pushes the balloon
in the opposite direction.
Jet action sends the balloon flying forward.

There is strong pressure inside rocket and
jet engines, too.

The pressure is built up when fuel is burned.
The burning fuel produces huge amounts of gas.
The gas pushes against the sides of the engine.

Some gas escapes through the tail-pipe opening.
The tail pipe is like the neck of your balloon.
The gas presses less in that direction.
But the rest of the gas keeps
pressing on the engine.
That pressure makes the rocket or plane
fly through the air.

Of course, your balloon zigzagged across the room.
It did not move like rockets and jets,
which fly a direct course.
Can you guess why?

Rockets have fins.
Jet planes also have wings and rudders.
The fins, wings, and rudders help to
steer the craft.

Here's a way to guide your balloon rocket.
Thread a long, thin string through
a drinking straw.
Make sure the straw can slide easily
along the string.
Tie one end of the string to a coat hanger.
Place the hanger on a coat hook or
some other object high in the room.

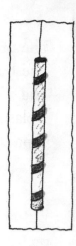

Stretch the string tight.
Tie the other end to a chair or table.
(Make sure the string is
free and clear of things in the room.)

Now blow up the balloon again.
Twist the neck a few times.
Seal it shut using a twist tie from
a plastic trash bag.
Tape the balloon to the straw.
(Make sure the neck is facing down.)

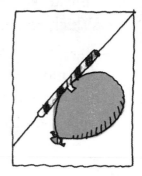

Count down slowly from 10 to 0.
At the same time, open the tie.
Then untwist the neck.
At zero, let go.
Watch your balloon zoom straight up
along the string.

Now run the string straight across the room
instead of from floor to ceiling.
Which way does the balloon travel farther?

You may notice that it goes farther
this way

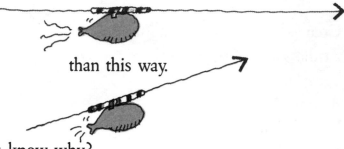

than this way.

Do you know why?
When the balloon flies up the string from
the floor, it is going against the force
of gravity.
Gravity pulls everything on earth down.
It slows the balloon as it travels up toward
the ceiling.

When you throw
a ball up
in the air, it
falls right down.
That's because
of gravity.

SIMPLE SCIENCE SAYS:
Make a Balloon Speedboat

Wash out an empty cardboard milk or juice container.
Push open the top to form a spout.
Put your scissors through the open spout.
Slide the scissors to where the spout
meets the glued-down part.

Cut down the front of the container.

Then cut down the back of the container.

Next, fold the bottom back and forth a few times.
This will make it easier to cut.
Now cut straight across the bottom.

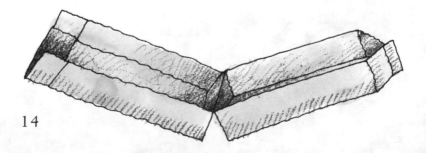

Throw away the half of the container with the spout.
You'll make your speedboat out of the part
with the sealed top.

Poke a small hole in the bottom part.
Thread the neck of the balloon through the hole.
Go from inside the boat to the outside.
Pull enough of the neck out so that you can
blow up the balloon.
Your balloon-powered speedboat is now ready
to be launched.

A shallow lake, pond, or stream is
a terrific place to try out your boat.
So is a big sink or wash basin with a stopper
to hold in the water.
Or you can use the bathtub — especially
at bath time.

Blow up the balloon.
Hold the neck closed
while you set the boat on the water.
Let go — and watch your speedboat take off!

What makes your balloon-speedboat zoom?
Jet action again!
The boat sails forward as the pressure
inside the balloon pushes in that direction.

Can you think of other ways to put
jet action to work for you?

Floating and Sinking

SIMPLE SCIENCE SAYS:
Make a Balloon Submarine

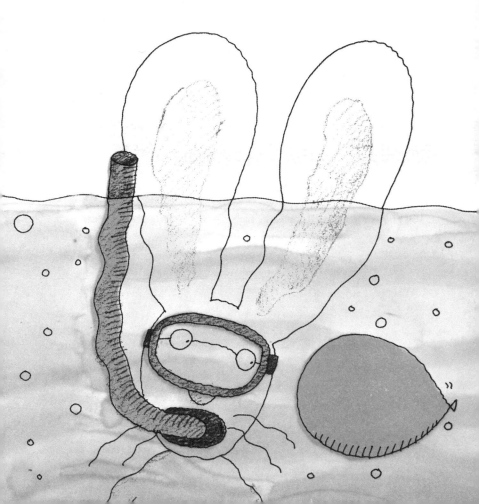

What happens when you put the balloon on water?
Will the balloon float on top of the water?
Or will it sink to the bottom?

The balloon floats because it is filled with air.
Air weighs less than water.
Anything that weighs less than water floats.

A piece of wood weighs less than water.
It floats.
A piece of steel weighs more than water.
It sinks.
But big ships are made of steel.
Why do they float?

Picture a large battleship.
It is mostly empty space on the inside.
In other words, the ship is filled with air.
Since air is lighter than water,
even heavy steel ships stay afloat.

Fit the neck of the balloon over a water tap.
Fill the balloon with water
and seal the neck with a twist tie.
The balloon now has its own weight
plus the weight of the water.
This makes the balloon slightly heavier
than the water alone.

Fill a sink with water and put the balloon in.
The balloon is not light enough to float
on top like a piece of wood.
But it is not heavy enough to sink
to the bottom like a piece of steel, either.
So the balloon stays just beneath
the surface of the water, like a submarine.

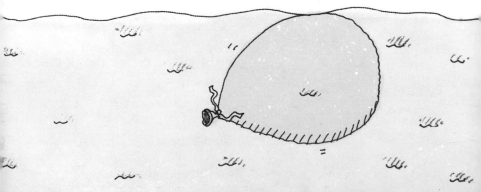

Now put the water-filled balloon under the tap.
Turn the tap on only about halfway
so water falls gently on top of the balloon.

Watch the balloon shake and jiggle.
Yet it stays in one place. It's trapped!
Why doesn't the force of the
falling water push it away?

Here's why.
The still water all around pushes in on the balloon.
The gently falling water doesn't press
as hard as still water.
Therefore, the still water keeps the balloon
in one place.

Turn off the tap.
Now there is nothing to hold the balloon back.
The balloon floats freely around in the water.

SIMPLE SCIENCE SAYS:
Make Balloon Bubbles

You will need a friend to help you with this activity.
First blow up your balloon.
Then pinch the neck together tightly.
Ask your friend to push the balloon under the water
as you hold on to the neck.
Now, still grasping the neck, let the air out.

Do you see a fountain of bubbles
come up through the water?
The bubbles are really the air
escaping from inside the balloon.
Air is lighter than water.
So the air rises to the top in the form of bubbles.

Try this neat trick with the balloon bubbles.
Get a small glass.
Ask your friend to place it in the water
until it fills up.
Then tell your friend to turn the glass upside down
while keeping it under the water.

The trick is to see if you can get
some of the water out of the glass —
but without taking it out of the water!

Here's how.
Blow up the balloon once again.
Push it down into the water and hold it
so the neck is under the glass.
Now let the air out.

Watch the bubbles of air go up into the glass.
Since air is lighter than water
it moves up into the glass.
And it pushes the water out.
Soon there is no water in the bottom
of the upside-down glass.

Can you think of other water activities
to do with your balloon?

24

Sound Vibrations

SIMPLE SCIENCE SAYS:
Make a Balloon Trumpet

Blow up the balloon.
Pinch the neck closed with both hands.
Make sure that no air escapes.
Now pull on the neck of the balloon,
letting out a tiny stream of air.
Do you hear the sound of your balloon trumpet?

Sounds are made when something shakes
back and forth very fast.
Vibration is another word for very fast shaking.

The air rushing out makes the neck of
the balloon vibrate.
And the vibrations produce the sound.

Blow up the balloon once more.
Let the air escape as you pull on the neck.
Do you hear the sound change?
The pitch goes lower.

Blow up the balloon again.
But this time bring your fingers together
as the air goes out.
Does the pitch go up or down?

When air escapes through a narrow opening,
the vibrations are fast.
The pitch is high, like a violin or flute.
But when the opening is wider,
the vibrations are slower.
The pitch goes down.
Then the balloon music sounds more like
a cello or tuba.

Practice making notes that go up and down the scale.
Then try to play a simple melody.
In time you might be able to play
"Yankee Doodle," "Mary Had a Little Lamb,"
or "Silent Night."

Static Electricity

SIMPLE SCIENCE SAYS:
Make an Electrical Balloon

Blow up the balloon and close it with a twist tie.
Now rub the balloon with a cloth made of wool.
Or rub the balloon on a woolen sweater,
coat, or rug.
Rub hard and fast for a few minutes.
This puts a charge of static electricity
on the balloon.

Hold the balloon over a mixture of salt and pepper
on a table. Watch it lift up the pepper,
and some of the salt, which is heavier.

Here are some other amazing things
you can do with your electrical balloon.
After trying each one, remember to rub the balloon
with wool again.
Rubbing builds up the electrical charge.

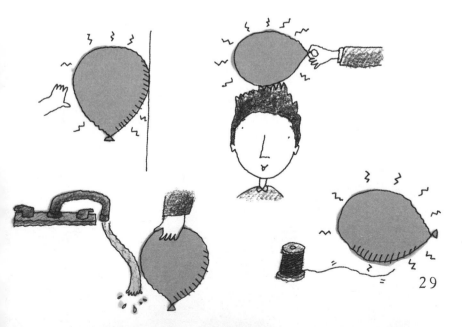

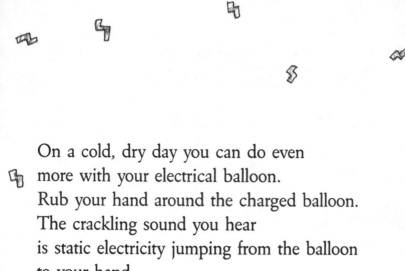

On a cold, dry day you can do even
more with your electrical balloon.
Rub your hand around the charged balloon.
The crackling sound you hear
is static electricity jumping from the balloon
to your hand.
In a dark room you may even see
tiny blue sparks fly between your hand
and the balloon.

Hot Air and Other Gases

SIMPLE SCIENCE SAYS:
Make a Hot-Air Balloon

Find a clean, empty glass bottle with a narrow neck.
Stretch the neck of the balloon
over the neck of the bottle.

Set the bottle in a small pot.
Add about two inches of water to the pot.
Place the pot on a stove.

Ask an adult to turn on the gas or
electricity under the pot.
As the water gets hot it warms the air
in the bottle.

Don't handle the
bottle when it is hot!

Turn off the
heat and let the
bottle cool first.

Soon the droopy balloon begins to wiggle.
It starts to puff out and become rounder.
In a little while,
the balloon is partly blown up.

Is this magic?
What blows up the balloon?

32

Air from inside the bottle does the trick.
The heat warms up the air in the bottle.
Hot air takes up more space than cold air.
There is no more room in the bottle.
So some of the hot air goes up
into the balloon.

You can do this same trick another way.
Place the bottle on a hot radiator.
The radiator is not as hot as the stove.
It will take longer for the balloon to blow up.
But after a while the hot air will move
from the bottle to the balloon.

SIMPLE SCIENCE SAYS:
Make a Gas-Filled Balloon

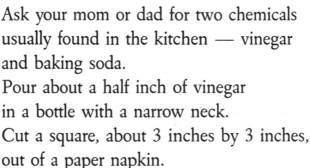

Ask your mom or dad for two chemicals
usually found in the kitchen — vinegar
and baking soda.
Pour about a half inch of vinegar
in a bottle with a narrow neck.
Cut a square, about 3 inches by 3 inches,
out of a paper napkin.
Place two tablespoons of baking soda
in the center of the square.
Fold the napkin over a few times.

Tie one end of a length of string around the napkin.
Lower the napkin into the bottle.
Stop when the napkin is just above —
but not touching — the vinegar.
Tie the top end of the string around
the bottleneck so the napkin hangs in place.

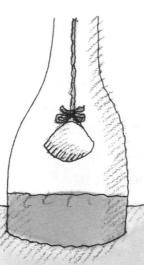

Now slip the neck of the balloon over
the bottle opening.
Shake the bottle back and forth very hard.
Make sure the vinegar splashes on the baking soda
in the napkin.

Do you see the vinegar bubble up?
It is giving off a gas.
The gas goes up into the balloon.
Soon the balloon stirs.
Before you know it, the balloon puffs up.

The trick works this way.
When baking soda and vinegar come together
they produce a gas called carbon dioxide.
The carbon dioxide fills the bottle.
But there's more gas here than the bottle can hold.
Some rises and blows up the balloon.

Smaller and Larger

SIMPLE SCIENCE SAYS:
Shrink Your Balloon

Blow up your balloon and close it tightly.
Tie a string snugly around the middle
of the balloon, like a belt around the waist.
Place the balloon into the freezer part
of your refrigerator.
Leave the balloon in the freezer for
ten or fifteen minutes.

Try to picture what is happening.
Is the balloon growing bigger,
and the string getting tighter?
Or is the balloon growing smaller,
and the string getting looser?
Or is everything staying the same?

You know that heat makes air take up more space.
The opposite is also true.
Cold makes air take up less space.
You can use your balloon to prove it!

When the time is up,
take the balloon out of the freezer.
What do you find?
The string is looser.
That means the balloon has grown smaller.
The freezer caused the air in the balloon
to take up less space.

Leave the balloon in the room for a while.
The room — we hope — is warmer than the freezer!
Watch the balloon return to its original size.
See how the string around the middle
gets snug again.

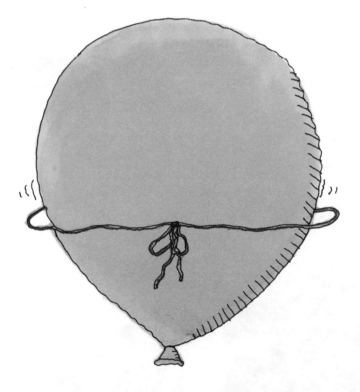

SIMPLE SCIENCE SAYS:
Make a Smelly Balloon

Do you know that a blown-up balloon is
losing air all the time —
even when it's tightly closed?
Here's a way to find out.

Before going to sleep, blow up the balloon.
Seal it very tightly so that no air leaks out
through the neck.
Tie a string snugly about its middle.
Place the balloon in a spot that is
just the right temperature — not too hot—or too cold.

Look at the balloon in the morning.
The string is looser. Some air escaped
through the solid skin of the balloon.

Here's another way to prove that air
passes through the balloon's skin.

You'll need a funnel and the help of a friend.
Have your friend slip the neck of the balloon
onto the funnel.

41

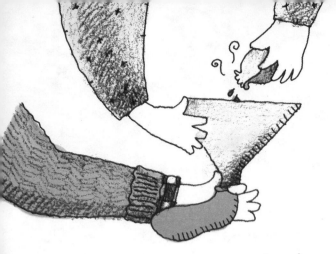

Put a couple of drops of some smelly
liquid inside the balloon.
Use liquid soap, cologne,
after-shave lotion, vinegar, or something else
with a strong scent.
Be careful not to drip any liquid
on the outside of the balloon.
Now blow air into the balloon.

After a few minutes, sniff the outside of the balloon.
You can probably smell the liquid.
The air — and the odor — sneaked out
through tiny, invisible openings in the skin
of the balloon.
This proves that the skin of a balloon
is not 100 percent airtight.

Get permission
from your
parents before
opening any
bottle of liquid.

Air Pressure

SIMPLE SCIENCE SAYS:
Make a Balloon Lift

Place your balloon on a table, desk, or shelf.
Let the neck of the balloon hang over the side.
Put a thick, heavy book on top of the balloon.
Now blow into the balloon.

While you're huffing and puffing,
keep your eyes on the book.
See it rise up off the table.
Congratulations!
You lifted a book without touching it!

Really, though, air pressure did the job.
This is how air pressure works.

When air is squeezed into a small space
it pushes to get out.
The air presses very hard on
whatever is holding it in.

When you blew up the balloon
you squeezed the air inside.
The air needed more room.
This built up the air pressure.
The pressure made the balloon larger —
and lifted up the book.

Suppose you are a detective.
You find a bottle with a wide neck.
It is an important clue in a murder case.
You don't want to touch the outside of the bottle.
It may have fingerprints.
You don't want to touch the inside of the bottle.
It may contain poison.
How can you carry the bottle to the crime lab?
Here's one way.

Stuff a balloon into the bottle
with the neck sticking out.
Blow up the balloon.

Now pick up the balloon by the neck.
The bottle lifts up at the same time!
Thanks to air pressure, you don't have
to touch the bottle — inside or out.

Here is an air-pressure trick
with a balloon and a bottle.
Try it on a friend.

You'll need an empty plastic or glass bottle
with a narrow neck.
Stuff the balloon into the bottle.
Let just the neck of the balloon stick out.
Now ask your friend to blow up the balloon.

Your friend may have very strong lungs.
But there is no way he or she can do it.

The clue is the bottle.
The bottle is filled with air.
Blowing up the balloon traps the air inside.
As the balloon grows bigger, it squeezes the air.
That builds up the air pressure
around the balloon.
The very strong pressure makes it impossible
to blow the balloon up all the way.

For another air-pressure trick,
get a clean, dry drinking glass.
Place the balloon inside the glass.
Blow up the balloon and twist the neck to seal it.
Hold it by the neck.

Ask some friends to try to pull the glass
off from the balloon.
They'll find it very hard to do.
In fact, they may not be able to do it at all.

The air pressure inside the balloon is very powerful.
It pushes with tremendous force against
the sides of the glass.
That's why it's so hard to get the glass off.
If someone pulls *very* hard, the balloon may even tear
before the glass comes off.

47

Can you think of other ways to put
the air pressure in a balloon to work for you?

There are so many ways you can have fun with balloons.
Balloons are truly amazing.

SIMPLE SCIENCE SAYS:
**Take One Balloon —
and see how far you can go!**